Contents

KETO SMOOTHIES COOKBOOK ....

    KETO SMOOTHIE RECIPE 8

        Ingredients 8

        Instructions 9

    KETO SMOOTHIE - BLUEBERRY 10

        Ingredients 10

        Instructions 10

    KETO SMOOTHIE 11

        INGREDIENTS 11

        DIRECTIONS 11

    PEANUT BUTTER KETO LOW CARB SMOOTHIE WITH ALMOND MILK 12

        Ingredients 12

        Instructions 13

    GREEN KETO SMOOTHIE 13

        Ingredients 13

        Instructions 14

    KETO CHOCOLATE MILKSHAKE 15

        INGREDIENTS 15

        INSTRUCTIONS 16

    KETO SMOOTHIE RECIPE 17

- INGREDIENTS 17
- INSTRUCTIONS 18
- KETO GREEN SMOOTHIE 18
  - Ingredients 18
  - Instructions 19
- STRAWBERRY KETO MILKSHAKE 20
  - Ingredients 20
  - Instructions 21
- KETO TRIPLE BERRY SMOOTHIE 21
  - Ingredients 21
  - Direction 22
- TRIPLE BERRY AVOCADO BREAKFAST SMOOTHIE 23
  - ingredients 23
  - Directions 23
- CHOCOLATE PEANUT BUTTER SMOOTHIE 24
  - Ingredients 24
  - Directions 24
- STRAWBERRY ZUCCHINI CHIA SMOOTHIE 25
  - Ingredients 25
  - Directions 25
- COCONUT BLACKBERRY MINT SMOOTHIE 26
  - Ingredients 26
  - Directions 26

LEMON CUCUMBER GREEN SMOOTHIE 26
    Ingredients 26
    Directions 27
CINNAMON RASPBERRY BREAKFAST SMOOTHIE..... 27
    Ingredients 27
    Directions 28
STRAWBERRIES AND CREAM SMOOTHIE................. 28
    Ingredients 28
    Directions 28
CHOCOLATE CAULIFLOWER BREAKFAST SMOOTHIE 29
    Ingredients 29
    Directions 30
PUMPKIN SPICE SMOOTHIE 30
    Ingredients 30
    Directions 31
KEY LIME PIE SMOOTHIE... 31
    Ingredients 31
    Directions 31
CHOCOLATE FAT BOMB SMOOTHIE 32
    Ingredients 32
    Instructions.. 33
KETO GOLDEN SMOOTHIE 33
    Ingredients 33

Instructions 34

Recipe Notes: 35

KETO MOCHA SMOOTHIE 35

Ingredients 35

Instructions 36

Recipe Notes: 37

KETO FLU SMOOTHIE 37

INGREDIENTS 37

INSTRUCTIONS 38

KETO MILKSHAKE SMOOTHIE WITH RASPBERRIES (LOW CARB) 39

INGREDIENTS 39

INSTRUCTIONS 40

VANILLA ICE CREAM KETO COFFEE SMOOTHIE 41

Ingredients 41

Instructions 42

FROSTED VANILLA BLACKBERRY LEMONADE 42

Ingredients 42

Instructions 43

Notes 44

HEALTHY CHOCOLATE PEANUT BUTTER LOW CARB SMOOTHIE RECIPE 44

INGREDIENTS 44

INSTRUCTIONS 45
SALTED CARAMEL KETO SMOOTHIE 46
   Ingredients 46
   Instructions 46
BLUEBERRY COCONUT CHIA SMOOTHIES 47
   Ingredients 47
   Instructions 48
VANILLA KETO SMOOTHIE 49
   Ingredients 49
   Instructions 50
COCONUT MILK STRAWBERRY SMOOTHIE 50
   Ingredients 50
   Instructions 50
MCKETO STRAWBERRY MILKSHAKE 51
   Ingredients 51
   Directions 51
VANILLA ALMOND KETO PROTEIN SHAKE 52
   INGREDIENTS 52
   INSTRUCTIONS 53
KETO SMOOTHIE - BLUEBERRY 53
   Ingredients 53
   Instructions 54
LOW-CARB FRUIT-FREE SMOOTHIE 54

Ingredients 54

Instructions... 55

KETO TROPICAL SMOOTHIE 56

Ingredients 56

Directions 57

BLUEBERRY COCONUT YOGURT SMOOTHIE RECIPE 57

Ingredients 57

INSTRUCTIONS.. 58

KETO CHOCOLATE SMOOTHIE................................ 58

Ingredients 58

Instructions... 59

AVOCADO MINT GREEN KETO SMOOTHIE................ 59

Ingredients 59

Instructions... 60

STRAWBERRY AVOCADO KETO SMOOTHIE RECIPE WITH ALMOND MILK 61

INGREDIENTS... 61

INSTRUCTIONS.. 62

LOW CARB BLUEBERRY PROTEIN POWER SMOOTHIE 62

Ingredients 62

Instructions... 63

MATCHA GREEN TEA SMOOTHIE 63

Ingredients 63

Instructions 64

CLEAN AND GREEN SMOOTHIE 64

Ingredients 64

Instructions 65

MINT COCO KETO SMOOTHIE 66

INGREDIENTS: 66

DIRECTIONS: 67

KETO CINNAMON ALMOND BUTTER BREAKFAST SHAKE 67

ingredients 67

instructions 68

KETO SMOOTHIES COOKBOOK

KETO SMOOTHIE RECIPE

Ingredients

- 1 cup ice

- 1 cup coconut milk beverage unsweetened (or preferred milk substitute)

- 1 cup spinach or dark leafy greens of choice

- 1 cup blackberries fresh or frozen

- 2 scoops whey protein isolate low carb, unflavored or flavor of choice, optional

- 1/2 tsp cinnamon

- 1/2 tsp vanilla extract

- monkfruit erythritol sweetener blend optional, to taste (or sweetener of choice)

Instructions

- Place all ingredients in a blender.

- Pulse ice crush setting until solid ingredients begin to breakdown. Change to purée setting until all ingredients are smoothly blended.

- Divide into individual serving sizes (240 g) to serve.

- Leftover mixture can be frozen in silicone molds and thawed for later use. Or freeze in popsicle molds for nutrient-dense popsicles!

KETO SMOOTHIE - BLUEBERRY

Ingredients

- 1 cup Coconut Milk or almond milk

- 1/4 cup Blueberries

- 1 tsp Vanilla Extract

- 1 tsp MCT Oil or coconut oil

- 30 g Protein Powder optional

Instructions

- Put all the ingredients into a blender, and blend until smooth.

KETO SMOOTHIE

INGREDIENTS

- 1 1/2 c. frozen strawberries

- 1 1/2 c. frozen raspberries, plus more for garnish (optional)

- 1 c. frozen blackberries

- 2 c. coconut milk

- 1 c. baby spinach

- Unsweetened shaved coconut, for garnish (optional)

DIRECTIONS

- In a blender, combine all ingredients (except for coconut). Blend until smooth.

- Divide between cups and top with raspberries and coconut, if using.

PEANUT BUTTER KETO LOW CARB SMOOTHIE WITH ALMOND MILK

Ingredients

- 1 Cup Almond Breeze Original Almondmilk

- 1 Cup Crushed ice

- 1/4 Cup Avocado (about 1/2 an avocado or 60g)

- 3 Tbsp Monkfruit, or to taste

- 2 Tbsp Natural creamy peanut butter (Almond butter for paleo)

- 1 Tbsp Unsweetened cocoa powder

Instructions

- Place all ingredients into a blender and blend until smooth.

- SLURP UP!

GREEN KETO SMOOTHIE

Ingredients

- 1 oz. kale leaves

- 1/2 avocado (peeled and stone removed)

- 1 stick celery (chopped)

- 2 oz. cucumber (peeled)

- 1 cup unsweetened almond milk (or regular milk)
- 1 tbsp. peanut butter (you can use any nut butter you like)
- 2 tbsp. freshly squeeze lemon juice

Instructions

- Add all of the ingredients to a high-speed blender.
- Pulse to combine, stopping to scrape down the sides if necessary.
- Serve immediately garnished with fresh mint or store in the fridge for later that day.

KETO CHOCOLATE MILKSHAKE

INGREDIENTS

- 1/2 cup full-fat coconut milk or heavy cream

- 1/2 medium avocado

- 1-2 tablespoons cacao powder to taste

- 1/2 teaspoon vanilla extract

- pinch pink Himalayan salt or salt of choice

- 2-4 tablespoons erythritol or sweetener of choice, to taste

- 1/2 cup ice as needed

- water as needed

OPTIONAL ADD-INS

- chia seeds ground (you'll need to add more water)

- MCT oil

- hemp hearts

- collagen peptides

- mint extract or extract of choice

INSTRUCTIONS

- Add coconut milk, avocado, cacao powder, vanilla extract, salt, sweetener and add-ins of choice to a blender (bullets work amazing here!).

- Blend until creamy smooth, using a little water as needed.

- Add in ice and blend until thick and creamy.

- Do not over-blend, or you'll lose thickness and coldness.

- Enjoy right away!

KETO SMOOTHIE RECIPE

INGREDIENTS

- 1 1/4 cups Thai Kitchen Coconut Milk

- 1 tsp low-carb sweetener — or more

- 1/4 avocado

- 1/2 cup blackberries

- 1 tsp chia seeds

- 2 tsp unsweetened cocoa powder

- 1 tsp peanut or almond butter

INSTRUCTIONS

- Place all ingredients in a blender and blend until smooth.

KETO GREEN SMOOTHIE

Ingredients

- handful / 15g kale

- handful / 10g fresh mint leaves, picked

- 0.25 avocado

- 0.13 / 50g fennel or 1 celery stick

- 0.13 small cucumber (100g)

- 0.5 tbsp protein powder unsweetened

- 0.5 cup / 240 ml almond milk unsweetened

- 0.5 tbsp almond butter

- 0.25 lemon, juiced

Instructions

- Scoop the avocado flesh out and place all ingredients into a high speed blender.

- Blend until smooth.

- Adjust thickness by adding more almond milk if desired.

Notes

- Protein powder is optional.

- You can replace the almond milk with coconut milk if you prefer.

- For a fruitier smoothie, add a handful of berries such as blueberries, strawberries or raspberries (plus 1 tsp or erythritol if you've got a sweet tooth). This will increase the carb count.

STRAWBERRY KETO MILKSHAKE

Ingredients

- 1/4 cup coconut milk such as Aroy-D or heavy whipping cream (60 ml/ 2 fl oz)

- 3/4 cup unsweetened almond milk or water (180 ml/ 6 fl oz)

- 1/2 cup strawberries, fresh or frozen (72 g/ 2.5 oz)

- 1 tbsp MCT oil or extra virgin coconut oil

- 1/2 tsp sugar-free vanilla extract

Instructions

- Place the coconut milk, almond milk, strawberries, ...

KETO TRIPLE BERRY SMOOTHIE

Ingredients

- 1/2 cup coconut milk

- 1.5 cups unsweetened almond milk

- 2/3 cup raspberries frozen

- 2/3 cup strawberries

- 1/2 cup blackberries

- 1 tbsp sugar free whipped cream optional

- Other optional add ins; low carb sweetener, collagen powder, protein powder, nut butter, MCT oil

Direction

- Place everything in a blender and process until smooth.

- If it's too thick add more coconut or almond milk, if it's too thin for your liking add in some ice and a little xanthan gum to thicken.

- Top with optional whipped cream if desired.

TRIPLE BERRY AVOCADO BREAKFAST SMOOTHIE

ingredients

- 1 cup (240 ml) of water

- 1/2 cup (98 grams) of frozen mixed berries (strawberries, blueberries, and raspberries)

- half of an avocado (100 grams)

- 2 cups (40 grams) of spinach

- 2 tablespoons (20 grams) of hemp seeds

Directions

- Combine the ingredients in a blender and blend until smooth.

CHOCOLATE PEANUT BUTTER SMOOTHIE

Ingredients

- 1 cup (240 ml) of unsweetened almond milk or another low-carb, plant-based milk

- 2 tablespoons (32 grams) of creamy peanut butter

- 1 tablespoon (4 grams) of unsweetened cocoa powder

- 1/4 cup (60 ml) of heavy cream

- 1 cup (226 grams) of ice

Directions

- Combine the ingredients in a blender and blend until smooth.

STRAWBERRY ZUCCHINI CHIA SMOOTHIE

Ingredients

- 1 cup (240 ml) of water

- 1/2 cup (110 grams) of frozen strawberries

- 1 cup (124 grams) of chopped zucchini, frozen or raw

- 3 tablespoons (41 grams) of chia seeds

Directions

- Combine the ingredients in a blender and blend until smooth.

COCONUT BLACKBERRY MINT SMOOTHIE

Ingredients

- 1/2 cup (120 ml) of unsweetened full-fat coconut milk

- 1/2 cup (70 grams) of frozen blackberries

- 2 tablespoons (20 grams) of shredded coconut

- 5–10 mint leaves

Directions

- Combine in a blender and blend until smooth.

LEMON CUCUMBER GREEN SMOOTHIE

Ingredients

- 1/2 cup (120 ml) of water

- 1/2 cup (113 grams) of ice

- 1 cup (130 grams) of sliced cucumber

- 1 cup (20 grams) of spinach or kale

- 1 tablespoon (30 ml) of lemon juice

- 2 tablespoons (14 grams) of milled flax seeds

Directions

- Combine in a blender and blend until smooth.

CINNAMON RASPBERRY BREAKFAST SMOOTHIE

Ingredients

- 1 cup (240 ml) of unsweetened almond milk

- 1/2 cup (125 grams) of frozen raspberries

- 1 cup (20 grams) of spinach or kale

- 2 tablespoons (32 grams) of almond butter

- 1/8 teaspoon of cinnamon, or more to taste

Directions

- Combine in a blender and blend until smooth.

STRAWBERRIES AND CREAM SMOOTHIE

Ingredients

- 1/2 cup (120 ml) of water

- 1/2 cup (110 grams) of frozen strawberries

- 1/2 cup (120 ml) of heavy cream

Directions

- Combine in a blender and blend until smooth.

CHOCOLATE CAULIFLOWER BREAKFAST SMOOTHIE

Ingredients

- 1 cup (240 ml) of unsweetened almond or coconut milk

- 1 cup (85 grams) of frozen cauliflower florets

- 1.5 tablespoons (6 grams) of unsweetened cocoa powder

- 3 tablespoons (30 grams) of hemp seeds

- 1 tablespoon (10 grams) of cacao nibs

- a pinch of sea salt

Directions

- Combine in a blender and blend until smooth.

PUMPKIN SPICE SMOOTHIE

Ingredients

- 1/2 cup (240 ml) of unsweetened coconut or almond milk

- 1/2 cup (120 grams) of pumpkin purée

- 2 tablespoons (32 grams) of almond butter

- 1/4 teaspoon of pumpkin pie spice

- 1/2 cup (113 grams) of ice

- a pinch of sea salt

Directions

- Combine in a blender and blend until smooth.

KEY LIME PIE SMOOTHIE

Ingredients

- 1 cup (240 ml) of water

- 1/2 cup (120 ml) of unsweetened almond milk

- 1/4 cup (28 grams) of raw cashews

- 1 cup (20 grams) of spinach

- 2 tablespoons (20 grams) of shredded coconut

- 2 tablespoons (30 ml) of lime juice

Directions

- Combine in a blender and blend until smooth.

CHOCOLATE FAT BOMB SMOOTHIE

Ingredients

- 2 ice cubes

- ½ cup (120mL) unsweetened coconut milk (from a carton)

- ¼ cup (60g) full-fat canned coconut cream

- 2 tbsp (24g) classic monk fruit sweetener

- 1 scoop (10g) MCT oil powder

- 1 tbsp (16g) No-Sugar-Added SunButter

- 1 tbsp (5g) unsweetened cocoa powder

- 1/16 tsp salt

Instructions

- To a high-speed blender, add all ingredients and pulse until smooth.

- Serve immediately and enjoy

KETO GOLDEN SMOOTHIE

Ingredients

- ¼ cup (60g) canned coconut cream

- 1 scoop (10g) MCT oil powder

- 1 tbsp (7g) freshly grated ginger

- 1 tbsp (12g) golden monk fruit sweetener

- ¾ tsp ground turmeric

- ½ tsp pure vanilla extract

- ⅛ tsp black pepper

- ⅛ tsp cinnamon

- 4 ice cubes

- ¼ cup + 2 tbsp (3 oz) cup water, divided

Instructions

- To a high-speed blender, add all ingredients excluding water.

- After all ingredients are added to blender and before turning blender on, pour in ¼ cup (2 oz) water and pulse until well-combined.

- Remove blender lid, pour in remaining 2 tbsp (1 oz) water, and blend again.

Recipe Notes:

- Coconut Substitution: For a coconut-free version, altogether omit the MCT oil powder and substitute heavy cream in for canned coconut cream at a 1:1 ratio. Note that the nutrition facts will change if you do this.

- Storage: Store smoothie in an airtight glass jar in the refrigerator and enjoy within 2 days.

KETO MOCHA SMOOTHIE

Ingredients

- ¼ cup + 2 tbsp (90 mL) heavy whipping cream

- ¼ cup (2 oz) water

- 2 tbsp (24g) classic monk fruit sweetener

- 2 tsp (3.3g) unsweetened cocoa powder

- 1 ¼ tsp (2.5g) espresso powder

- 1/16 tsp salt

- 4 ice cubes

- Optional:

- 1 scoop (10g) MCT oil powder

Instructions

- To a high-speed blender, add all ingredients and pulse until just combined, being careful to not over-blend, which will lead to the smoothie being too thin.

Recipe Notes:

- For A Dairy-Free, Vegetarian, and Vegan Recipe: Substitute canned coconut cream for heavy whipping cream at a 1:1 ratio.

- For A Coconut-Free Recipe: If you have a coconut allergy or intolerance, simply omit the optional ingredient of MCT Oil Powder, which contains coconut.

- Storage: Store smoothie in an airtight glass jar in the refrigerator and enjoy within 2 days.

KETO FLU SMOOTHIE

INGREDIENTS

- 1/2 cup Kale

- 2 large Strawberries

- 50 grams Avocado

- 1/2 cup Cucumber, with peel

- 1/2 cup Unsweetened Almond Milk

- 1 tsp Stevia

- 1 tsp Vanilla Extract

- 1/2 tsp Pink Himalayan Salt

INSTRUCTIONS

- Add all ingredients to a blender. Blend until smooth. Chill or pour over ice.

KETO MILKSHAKE SMOOTHIE WITH RASPBERRIES (LOW CARB)

INGREDIENTS

- 1 cup unsweetened plain almond milk

- 1 cup crushed ice

- 1/4 cup heavy whipping cream

- 1/4 cup fresh raspberries

- 2 tbsp confectioners swerve or sweetener of choice

- 1 tbsp cream cheese

- 1/2 tsp vanilla extract

- pinch of salt (<1/8 teaspoon)

INSTRUCTIONS

- Microwave cream cheese in a small bowl for about 5 seconds or until soft.

- Add all ingredients to a blender (I use a Nutribullet).

- Blend until very smooth.

- Taste and adjust accordingly by adding more Serve for a sweeter taste, or another tablespoon of cream cheese for a creamier finish. If using a different sweetener, add it to taste.

- Serve immediately. If not served right away, keep chilled in an ice bath. Separation is normal so give it a stir before drinking.

VANILLA ICE CREAM KETO COFFEE SMOOTHIE

Ingredients

- 3.75 oz Death Wish Coffee or strong coffee frozen into ice cubes

- 1.5 cups unsweetened vanilla almond milk

- 1 tbsp Perfect Keto MCT Oil

- 1 tbsp chia seeds

- 2 tbsp heavy whipping cream

- 1 tsp vanilla extract

- 1/8 tsp stevia

Instructions

- Freeze coffee in an ice cube tray. (12 oz coffee will fill a standard ice cube tray.)

- Note: If you don't use Death Wish Coffee, you will need to use more coffee cubes if you want the same caffeine content.

- Add all ingredients to a blender and blend until smooth.

- Pour in a glass.

FROSTED VANILLA BLACKBERRY LEMONADE

Ingredients

- 2/3 cup unsweetened almond or cashew milk

- 1/4 cup lemon juice

- 1 tablespoon collagen

- ½ teaspoon Now Better Stevia Extract

- 2 pinches Himalayan salt or Mineral Salt

- 1 teaspoon vanilla extract

- ½ teaspoon glucomannan

- 1/2 cup blackberries, fresh or frozen

- 3 cups ice cubes (around one full tray)

Instructions

- Put lemon juice, almond milk, collagen, stevia, salt, and vanilla in blender.

- Turn on low for just a few seconds to mix.

- While blender is on low, slowly add in glucomannan.

- Blend on low for 30 seconds and turn off.

- Add in blackberries and ice cubes, blend on high until completely blended.

Notes

- Depending on the sweetness of your blackberries, you may need to add a bit more sweetener.

HEALTHY CHOCOLATE PEANUT BUTTER LOW CARB SMOOTHIE RECIPE

INGREDIENTS

- 1/4 cup Peanut butter (creamy)

- 3 tbsp Cocoa powder

- 1 cup Heavy cream (or coconut cream for dairy-free or vegan)

- 1 1/2 cup Unsweetened almond milk (regular or vanilla)

- 6 tbsp Powdered erythritol (to taste)

- 1/8 tsp Sea salt (optional)

INSTRUCTIONS

- Combine all ingredients in a blender.

- Puree until smooth. Adjust sweetener to taste if desired.

SALTED CARAMEL KETO SMOOTHIE

Ingredients

- 1 bag Bigelow Salted Caramel Tea steeped in 6 oz. water

- 1 cup unsweetened almond milk

- 2 tbsp whipping cream

- 1 tbsp MCT oil

- 1/2 tsp stevia

- 3/4 tsp xanthan gum

- 8 ice cubes

Instructions

- Steep 1 bag of Bigelow Salted Caramel Tea in 6 oz. water.

- Remove and discard tea bag when done.

- Combine remaining ingredients in a blender and blend until smooth. (Pour into a glass and serve.

BLUEBERRY COCONUT CHIA SMOOTHIES

Ingredients

- 1 cup frozen blueberries

- 1 cup full fat Greek yogurt (you can use almond milk or coconut milk yogurt for dairy-free and vegan options)

- 1/2 cup coconut cream (the really thick creamy stuff from the top of the can of full fat coconut milk)

- 1 cup unsweetened cashew or almond milk

- 2 tbsp coconut oil

- 2 tbsp ground chia seed

- 2 Tbsp Swerve Sweetener or equivalent sweetener (use your favourite)

- Feel free to add protein powder, collagen or any other supplement that appeals to you.

Instructions

- Combine all ingredients in blender and blend until smooth.

- Divide among 4 glasses and serve.

VANILLA KETO SMOOTHIE

Ingredients

- 2 large eggs

- 1/2 cup soured cream or coconut milk such as Aroy-D (120 ml/ 4 fl oz)

- 1/4 cup vanilla or plain whey protein or collagen powder (25 g/ 0.9 oz)

- 1 tbsp MCT oil or extra virgin coconut oil (15 ml)

- seeds from 1 vanilla bean or 1 tsp sugar-free vanilla extract

- 3-5 drops Stevia extract

- 1/4 cup water + few ice cubes

Instructions

- Place the soured cream, whey protein powder and water into a blender.

COCONUT MILK STRAWBERRY SMOOTHIE

Ingredients

- 1 cup strawberries frozen

- 1 cup unsweetened coconut milk

- 2 tablespoons smooth almond butter

- 2 packets stevia optional

Instructions

- Add all ingredients to blender.

- Blend until smooth.

- Pour into glass and enjoy

MCKETO STRAWBERRY MILKSHAKE

Ingredients

- ¾ cup coconut milk (from the carton)

- ¼ cup heavy whipping cream

- 7 large ice cubes

- 2 tablespoons Sugar-free Strawberry Torani

- 1-2 tablespoons MCT oil

- ¼ teaspoon xanthan gum

Directions

- Add all ingredients to your blender.

- Blend everything together for 1-2 minutes or until the consistency is good for you.

- Pour out and enjoy

VANILLA ALMOND KETO PROTEIN SHAKE

INGREDIENTS

- 1-2 avocados

- 2 tbsp almond butter

- 1 tbsp MCT Oil

- 1 cup almond milk

- 1 cup frozen cauliflower

- 1 tbsp vanilla

- 1 scoop chocolate protein powder (optional)

- stevia (to taste)

- Vanilla Almond Keto Protein Shake

INSTRUCTIONS

- Put all ingredients together in a blender. Blend until pureed.

KETO SMOOTHIE - BLUEBERRY

Ingredients

- 1 cup Coconut Milk or almond milk

- 1/4 cup Blueberries

- 1 tsp Vanilla Extract

- 1 tsp MCT Oil or coconut oil

- 30 g Protein Powder optional

Instructions

- Put all the ingredients into a blender, and blend until smooth.

LOW-CARB FRUIT-FREE SMOOTHIE

Ingredients

- 1 cup unsweetened almond milk

- 1/2 avocado

- 1-2 cups spinach

- 1/2 scoop protein powder, I use Plant Fusion

- 1 tsp cocoa powder

- 1 Tbsp hemp seeds

- 1 Tbsp MCT oil
- 10 drops liquid stevia
- 1/4 - 1/2 cup water for thinning out to desired consistency
- Ice cubes
- 1 tsp cacao nibs (optional)

Instructions

- Add all the ingredients except cacao nibs to a blender and blend on high until smooth.
- Pour into a glass and sprinkle with cacao nibs.
- Sip and enjoy

KETO TROPICAL SMOOTHIE

Ingredients

- 7 large ice cubes

- ¾ cup unsweetened coconut milk

- ¼ cup sour cream

- 2 tablespoons golden flaxseed meal

- 1 tablespoon MCT Oil

- 20 drops liquid Stevia

- ½ teaspoon mango extract

- ¼ teaspoon blueberry extract

- ¼ teaspoon banana extract

Directions

- Add all ingredients together into a blender.

- Blend for 1-2 minutes until everything is incorporated well, then serve up

BLUEBERRY COCONUT YOGURT SMOOTHIE RECIPE

Ingredients

- 1 pot (120 ml) of coconut yogurt

- 10 blueberries

- 1 cup coconut milk

- 1/2 teaspoon vanilla extract (omit for AIP)

- Stevia to taste (omit for AIP)

INSTRUCTIONS

- Place all the ingredients into the blender and blend really well.

- Enjoy for a quick and nutritious breakfast or snack.

KETO CHOCOLATE SMOOTHIE

Ingredients

- 1can full fat coconut milk (375 grams)

- ¼cup egg white protein powder (20 grams)

- 2tablespoons ground chia seeds (20 grams)

- ½teaspoon vanilla stevia

- ⅓cup chopped 85% dark chocolate (50 grams)

- 2-3cups ice

Instructions

- In a vitamix, combine coconut milk, protein powder, chia, and stevia

- Blend in chocolate until smooth

- Blend in ice cubes until mixture is well combined

- Serve

AVOCADO MINT GREEN KETO SMOOTHIE

Ingredients

- 1/2 of an avocado (about 3-4 ounces)

- 3/4 cup full fat coconut milk

- 1/2 cup almond milk

- low carb sugar substitute to taste

- 5-6 large mint leaves

- 3 sprigs of cilantro

- 1 squeeze of lime juice

- ¼ tsp vanilla

- 1 – 1 1/2 cup crushed ice

Instructions

- Place all of the ingredients except the ice into the blender.

- Blend on low speed until completely pureed.

- Add the crushed ice and blend.

- Taste to adjust sweetness and tartness.

- Serve.

STRAWBERRY AVOCADO KETO SMOOTHIE RECIPE WITH ALMOND MILK

INGREDIENTS

- 1 lb Frozen strawberries

- 1 1/2 cups Almond Breeze Original Almond Milk

- 1 large Avocado

- 1/4 cup Powdered allulose (or other powdered sweetener of choice - adjust amount to taste)

- Wholesome Yum Keto Sweeteners

INSTRUCTIONS

- Puree all ingredients in a blender, until smooth.

Adjust sweetener to taste as needed.

LOW CARB BLUEBERRY PROTEIN POWER SMOOTHIE

Ingredients

- ¼ cup fresh blueberries

- 1 tbs flaxseed meal

- 8 oz unsweetened almond milk

- 1 scoop vanilla whey protein

- low carb simple syrup, optional

Instructions

- Mix all ingredients in a jug blender or immersion blender, and blend until smooth.

- Test for sweetness and add syrup as desired.

MATCHA GREEN TEA SMOOTHIE

Ingredients

- 3/4 cup unsweetened almond milk or coconut milk

- 1 tablespoon chia seeds

- 1 teaspoon matcha green tea powder

- 1/4 teaspoon lemon juice

- 5 drops vanilla stevia drops

- 2 tablespoons plain whole milk Greek yogurt use coconut cream for dairy free

- 1/4 teaspoon glucomannon or xanthan gum (optional thickeners)

- 1/4 cup crushed ice optional

Instructions

- Combine all ingredients with blender until smooth.

CLEAN AND GREEN SMOOTHIE

Ingredients

- 1 cup filtered water

- 1/2 avocado

- 1 tablespoon MCT oil (Simply Good Fats)
- 1/2 organic cucumber
- 1 large handful dark leafy greens
- 1 – 2 leaves dandelion
- 2 tablespoons parsley
- 2 tablespoons hemp seeds
- Juice from 1 lemon
- ¼ teaspoon turmeric powder or 2 turmeric capsules

Instructions

- Blend all ingredients in a high-speed blender until smooth, about 1 minute.
- Best enjoyed cold.

MINT COCO KETO SMOOTHIE

INGREDIENTS:

- 4oz full fat coconut milk
- 4oz water
- 1/2 cup frozen cauliflower
- 1/2 avocado
- 1 scoop collagen protein
- 1 tsp vanilla extract
- 1 tbsp chopped mint
- 1 tbsp cacao powder
- 1 tbsp coconut oil

- dash of ceylon cinnamon

- dash of himalayan sea salt

- optional toppings coconut flakes, chia seeds, flaxseeds, hemp seeds, pumpkin seeds, sliced macadamia nuts

DIRECTIONS:

- Throw all ingredients into a blender and blend until very smooth and creamy. Enjoy!

KETO CINNAMON ALMOND BUTTER BREAKFAST SHAKE

ingredients

- 1 1/2 cups unsweetened nut milk

- 1 scoop collagen peptides
- 2 Tbsp almond butter
- 2 Tbsp golden flax meal
- ½ tsp cinnamon
- 15 drops liquid stevia
- 1/8 tsp almond extract
- 1/8 tsp salt
- 6–8 ice cubes

instructions

- Add all the ingredients to a blender and combine for 30 seconds or until you get a smooth consistency.

Printed in Great Britain
by Amazon